Sup Me

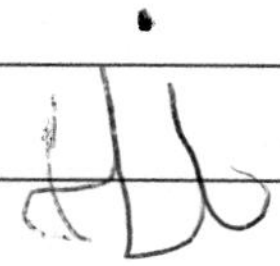

Made in the USA
Columbia, SC
28 May 2023

17444519R00055